Liquid Paper

Also by Peter Meinke

FICTION
The Piano Tuner, 1986

POETRY
The Night Train and the Golden Bird, 1977
Trying to Surprise God, 1981
Night Watch on the Chesapeake, 1987

POETRY CHAPBOOKS
Lines from Neuchâtel, 1974
The Rat Poems, 1978
Underneath the Lantern, 1986
Far from Home, 1989

CHILDREN'S VERSE
The Legend of Larry the Lizard, 1969
Very Seldom Animals, 1970

CRITICISM
Howard Nemerov, 1968

Liquid Paper

New and Selected Poems

PETER MEINKE

University of Pittsburgh Press

Pittsburgh • London

The publication of this book is supported by grants from the National
Endowment for the Arts in Washington, D.C., a Federal agency, and the
Pennsylvania Council on the Arts.

Published by the University of Pittsburgh Press, Pittsburgh, Pa. 15260
Copyright © 1991, Peter Meinke
All rights reserved
Eurospan, London
Manufactured in the United States of America

Library of Congress Cataloging-in-Publication Data

Meinke, Peter.
    Liquid paper : new and selected poems / Peter Meinke.
       p.   cm. — (Pitt poetry series)
   ISBN 0–8229–3681–X (cl).—ISBN 0–8229–5455–9 (pb.)
   I. Title. II. Series.
PS3563.E348L56 1991
811'.54—dc20   91-50108
                                                  CIP

A Cip catalogue record for this book is available from the British Library.

Most of these new poems have appeared in magazines, among them *America,
Clockwatch Review, Grand Street, The New Republic, New Virginia Review,
Poetry, Religion & Intellectual Life, Tampa Review, West Branch, Yankee,* and
others.

"Easter in Neuchâtel" first appeared in a chapbook, *Far from Home,*
published by Heatherstone Press, 1989.

Thanks to the National Endowoment for the Arts for a fellowship in
creative writing for 1989, during which most of the new poems were
written; and to Davidson College for appointing me the McGee Writer-in-
Residence during the spring of 1989 when I was working on this book.

Cover art: "A Poet's Paradise: Portrait for My Father," by Perrie Meinke,
1978.

for Kiara Jeanne
born April 19, 1991

Contents

Liquid Paper

Liquid Paper

Smooth as a snail, this little parson
pardons our sins. Touch the brush tip
lightly and—*abracadabra!*—a clean slate.

We know those who blot their brains
by sniffing it, which shows
it erases more than ink
and with imagination anything
can be misapplied . . . In the army,
our topsergeant drank aftershave, squeezing
my Old Spice to the last slow drop.

It worked like Liquid Paper in his head

until he'd glide across the streets of Heidelberg
hunting for the house in Boise, Idaho,
where he was born. . . . If I were God
I'd authorize Celestial Liquid Paper
every seven years to whiten our mistakes:
we should be sorry and live with what we've done
but seven years is long enough and all of us

deserve a visit now and then
to the house where we were born
before everything got written so far wrong.

I. New Poems

Father

My father's eyes rolled upward in Paul's Diner,
not in fine frenzy but diabetic coma

and we thought when they refocused two weeks
later it was time to make amends. We

had circled one another for fifty years,
he round as a sumo wrestler, I blind

as a blinkered horse: we couldn't get a grip.
I remember now the smell of his sweat

as we dug boulders for the fence out back
and how later in the ball game he stuck

out his arm at home plate and my tall friend
folded across it like laundry on a line

and let me tell you, old man, I was proud
at having the strongest father on the block.

The Dead Tree

Last spring you said
it's an ancient mariner,
this white ash poised

like a spar among
the flat-footed maples,
bare arms upborne,

diver in perfect form.
Now it's late June
and the mountain

swims in green
but the ash stands gray
and rigid against the wind

like driftwood
whipped by seaweed
in the eddying shoals.

Our neighbors say
Cut it down
for its straight grain

and pure line—but
we're not finished yet:
nature includes its dead.

A wren's nest, a squirrel's
shortcut, brief rest
in a monarch's long trek:

this ash is more
than timber—and you,
father, anchor

and keel, sing
in the rigging
as the ship sails on.

Soldiers with Green Leggings

—Villa Schifanoia, 1987

Father and daughter marched between
the erect cypresses, moss turning

the dark trunks green
on the north side

like soldiers with green leggings
and he wanted to say

Let us lay down our swords
(how pompous like a father!)

and she wanted to say
Let's open our doors

(how sentimental like a daughter!)
but the music in their heads

kept playing so they held
their chins high, stepping

together left right left right
smart as any parade and soon

the trees marched with them
ground rumbling like distant cannon

birds whirling like bewildered
messengers until a white flag

rose from the castle
and they fell to their knees

to sign the treaty:
any treaty—my treaty, your treaty.

Growing Deaf

Underwater, I could still hear music,
the shrill cries of my friends, the school
bus clearing its oily throat: muted
voices wavered by my ear, like sunfish
gossiping near the dock or small-mouth bass
coughing in the shadows.

I circled toward the beach, trying to escape
the killer arm of Freddy Kollmorgen, but
surfaced six feet from him, looking the wrong way.
He fired the waterlogged tennis ball, heavy
as kryptonite, knocking me over
like a cardboard duck—

and something broke. My left ear hammering,
I limped through drums up the beach, slid
on my bike and pedaled home. Thirteen
and ignorant of pain, I curled in bed
until my sister screamed,
the pillowcase soaked in blood . . .

. . . *Today, leaning from habit my right ear in,*
everything sounds underwater now—your coral laughter,
my friends mouthing like trout—and I remember
Freddy Kollmorgen, imagine him pitching to his grandson,
the boy round-eyed, waving his plastic bat,
indestructible . . .

The Perch

That day in the canoe
the summer sun poured down
like angel butter and I sat
for hours without a nibble,
the lake flat as a fry pan.
Only the limp, torn cardboard
of last night's celebrations
disturbed the surface until
my bobber lurched, the pole
humped, and I pulled
a yellow perch into the fifth of July.

Plump as a pillow—
but too little and too late
to make a meal for us—
he'd swallowed the bait
and his scarlet gills gaped
like knife wounds
as I twisted the crooked hook
to yank it out, his barred
bloodshot breast snapping,
and I cut my hand on his fins
before dropping him in the lake.

It was still ninety degrees
at the dock when I shouldered
the canoe, staggering up our steep
steps—and suddenly my breath
blew from my lungs, the Adirondacks swirled
around me, a red wire circled
my chest and flung me to the ground,
the canoe pinning my leg like a worm
near the rack. Someone
held me over the edge of something—
and threw me back.

Fixed Stars

—for Lauren & Suzy Yoder

On our left, Orion's belt curves above the barn.
On our right the Big Dipper tilts
toward the huge shark-shaped rock the children
call Jaws. We can see why Aristotle
thought the world a dome, the fixed stars
scrolling across heaven like notes
in a player piano. I say "I can almost
hear the music," and Lauren says, "Pass
the bottle and maybe I'll hear it, too."

The music's a mix of Turtlefish Brook
and the wind skimming across an ocean
of pine, ghostly sonata blowing over
the Yoder's cabin, anchored on Brainard Ridge.
The children sleep, convinced we won't spin
into space or sink like a weighted coffin
dropped overboard to the fish. They love
stories that scare them to death: "Tell us,"
Tim whispered, "'The Man Who Was Buried Alive' . . ."

The earth's shadow on the moon is always round—
that's how Aristotle knew the world's not
flat as a table with edges that sailors fall off,
floating forever in circles ordained by the gods,
their women stubbornly weaving in emptying towns.
But now the gods themselves lie down in the bellies
of endangered whales, the dome rolled back
while telescopes like enormous cannons pick off
the fast fading stars and leave the sky black.

All week I've had trouble breathing. Just asthma,
we hope, and indeed milkweed and goldenrod
nodding in loose constellations surround us,

uncountable clusters and clots in every direction.
In an infinite universe each is the logical
center, the stars no longer fixed but swimming
away like trout when the shadow approaches, leaving
us there alone when it arrives—in the middle
of everything, knowing nothing about it.

Easter in Neuchâtel

The rosy-fingered dawn
is at it again, I said. You said,
pouring our coffee, Let's believe
in home and Homer. Just then
the clouds were lifting and the Alps
in morning splendor raised their heads,
or hoods, like God's own cowlèd monks.

Hosanna! Hosanna!
Our mountains nudge us to believe
in something, the romantic
wishbone aching like Grandma's wrist
before a rain. Beyond our sight,
on clumps of rocks and chunks
of mountainside, rosettes

of saxifrage and campanula
cling in their pure design
celebrating spring. It's Easter!
and the whitewashed Alps, baptized
by the vernal equinox,
chart in jagged graph our dizzying swing
between the movable peaks of faith and feast.

Indigo Buntings

This summer, four buntings govern
our lives, pulling us from window
to door, so we've named them for the
four forces of the universe:

Weak, Strong, EM, and Gravity.
Weak is the male, of course, warbling
his handsome head off, in sunshine
a Mediterranean blue,

an example of diffraction
and deception—he's really black.
The female, Strong, feeding their young,
matches the brown cup of their nest;

we like to think she's defying
Gravity, the pushy one, drop-
ping thistle seeds in the thin throat
of his sister, EM—perhaps

we're wrong in this . . . We know the world
is sick and eats its young: but when
our grandchild visits there they are,
four buntings, ungrounded on our
wires, practicing their scales; they
repeat their high repeated notes—
sweet-sweet, see-it see-it, sweet-sweet—
while we teach Caitlin all their names:

"Tell them 'Bye-bye Baby Bunting,' "
we say. She stares wide-eyed with up-
turned face, the forces holding us
momentarily all in place:

these are our grace notes, full of grace.

The Anniversary Deer

—for Doug & Karin Clark

Returning at dawn from the city
and your thirty-fifth anniversary, tight
on talk and champagne and the scene on the train,
we surprised on our lawn three deer—a doe,
a buck, and a fawn.

You who have dreamed your lives in symbols
would have nodded: the deer framed by our lights,
our transported selves not daring to drive
another inch or break the spell—all
around us contriving

to hold that moment motionless, as God
froze the sun for Joshua—so we counted
twelve round stones in our driveway, knowing
some omen beckoned, the stones glinting like spilled
subway tokens . . .

and then the last star pulled out of the sky, the doe
shuffled her magical legs like Pick Up
Stix, and they were gone. I started the car,
leaves began feathering down, and the sun
began warming

(we worried) souvenirs left by the deer: ticks
whose bites drive us mad as the shaking man
on the subway tonight: *God has His tricks—*
he was howling—*in heaven the rich will be hooked
and beg for a fix . . .*

Something like that. You both would have emptied
your pockets and taken his hand. Surely (we reasoned)
the deer were sent to tell us: in spite
of madness, disease, and the stench of corruption
sticking tight

to all that we touch, there remain times
when doors slide open and innocence waits
like a clean train. Such a bright sign
on your thirty-fifth anniversary must mean
at least that much . . .

The Shell

—for Gretchen

wasn't perfect, a few chips and holes,
but its contours whorled
powderfine to the touch, insides
smooth as pink glass. *Take it,*

my father said, *listen.*
What do you hear?
I was a city girl, age three
or four, and suspicious, but as I
pressed it to my ear the sound
came clear, and I said *Daddy, guess what?*
They've got the air-conditioner on!

That's a story we still tell, and
I remember how, later, my life
spiraling under the sun, they told me
it was the roar of the sea
and I believed that too, hearing wind
and wave and seeing with romantic eye
the frantic wake, the frail and shaken ships.

Then in my student years I learned
what I heard was my own blood
on its own dark road, carrying
secret messages of help or distress
from station to station, the shell
an echo chamber I studied intensely,
trying to break the code.

And now, these moonlit years,
I see my blood inseparable
from the world's, and the shell's voice
sings on the tide of all living things

lonely in darkened rooms, lost at sea
listening through fog for the sound of bells,
huddled in fear of soldier or sailor;

and I take our child down to the shore
to hunt for shells . . .

Minuet in G

Certain melodies can break your heart
just seeing them on the page, their plump ovals
bobbing like sea gulls on the surface
of some moonless tide . . .

                  and this bent corner
conjures the broad hand of Mr. Herbert whose
crescented thumbnail seemed wide as my wrist
when he pressed it down, saying, *Next week, Peter,*
we make acquaintance with Mr. Ludwig
van Beethoven, my mother hovering,
tugging her slender fingers as if to say
Grow, Peter, you can do it, concentrate,
while outside my friends whooped,
slapping a bald tennis ball against our stoop,
Mr. Herbert murmuring *Legato, legato,*
and I dreaming gondoliers
and black-haired women with shadowy cleavage
leaning from balconies, singing my name,
Pietro, Pietro . . .

                the notes
on their frail stems still skittering
in clusters down the yellowing page
like children playing "3 Steps to Germany"
in Brooklyn, one December evening, 1941.

Talk of the Paintings

At night the paintings roll up their colors
like ribbons and slide from their frames
pale as "Casablanca," visiting in the dark.
Mon Dieu, shouts Déjeuner,
are the women getting skinny or what?
Ach, mein freund, says Bathsheba,
they are not loved, I hear them, there
is no time—business, always business.

Monkey business, if you ask me, says Mona Lisa,
laughing out loud, *Ciao, amica.*

O the paintings gossip by the fountain,
a convention of flower-loving nudists,
of rich merchants and warriors,
their vowels and consonants mounting
in a babel of pure sound
meaning absolutely nothing.
The museum is relaxed, happy—
and then the doors open.

The paintings hear your footsteps. They tense.
You turn and they explode in light.

Arms and the Man

At the Publix counter, she lifts the plastic
bag with a grunt, and her elbow puckers
like a dimpled sock. By the automatic
doors a man-sized scale stares her down
as she shuffles by, guilty on all counts.

Her car's parked far in the lot because
she can't get it into reverse; it coughs
like her mother when the motor stops,
and in the house the dog her sister sent
to keep her company has chewed the photo
album she forgot to put away. Fuck it.
She pours her first drink of the day.

O muse of ships and tides, lunar ghost,
rose of deepening shadows, long-fingered
comforter, what have we done? Across
America hosts of dumpy women slump
in musty kitchens, dying of silence.

No one to talk to, abandoned by sullen men
who drive down Main Streets uglier than Belsen,
surrounded by cement and wires and lies
pervasive as polluted air, husband father
son brother strung out along the All-American line:
silence at one end violence
at the other.

She wrote poetry in high school, and dreamed
The Dream, humorless and perfect, patriotic
as Barbie; now she talks to her dog
while watching Donahue and when high enough
will telephone her oldest friend and cry.

O great-winged Furies, send us no more he-men
riding wordlessly toward manly epitaphs, but
in their place deliver those who talk and listen,
distrust perfection and the seamless young;
who will hang around, for god's sake, love
their women better than any hero, and kiss
the inside of their thickening arms and laugh.

Progress

We are mind!
cried old Descartes,
and Wordsworth countered,
No, we're heart.

Down a new road
at last we come.
Our code: *Libido*
ergo sum.

Exodus with Children

She was searching for a sign and listening
for a word while Ohio unrolled beneath
the old Mustang: Piketon, Waverly, Alma,
Chillicothe, Kinnikinnick—maybe the Indians
could have helped, if they were still around:
Do not move until Spring Moon, wash three times
in the Olentangy, name the children Fire Heart,
White Fox, Eagle Feather. Now they were singing
their school's fight song, voices like snow crystals
clinging to the ends of branches. A new school
waited, somewhere, new teams to cheer: truly
American now, displaced, on the move.
Five miles before Columbus, starlings swooped
and swerved in huge flocks, God's tribal flash cards.

Myth

On Seventh Avenue, once upon
one afternoon in April two
cars fleeing in opposite directions
stopped at the light. Suddenly

their doors flared open, a man
and a woman ran from the cars
and embraced on the thin median
between the lanes. She was crying. He was

crying. The light changed
while they held each other, crying, on
the green plastic strip of the median.
There was some honking at first

that died down as drivers, transported,
stared at the couple. For a while
the ice cream man came by, and
children, wondering. . . . In time,

a policeman strode up, but stopped
six steps away, hand on nightstick—
and slowly a terrific silence fell like
green snow, weeds and ivy creeping

over bumpers
and plastic grass
as the cars settled, sighing,
on their rusting rims.

And finally, the city itself
had to be abandoned, though who the lovers were
and why they cried like that, no one,
not even the mayor, ever discovered.

Love Poem 1990

When I was young and shiny as an apple in the good Lord's garden
I loved a woman whose beauty like the moon moved all the
      humming heavens to music
till the stars with their tiny teeth burst into song
and I fell on the ground before her while the sky hardened
and she laughed and turned me down softly, I was so young.

When I was a man sharp as a polished axe in the polleny orchard
I loved a woman whose perfume swayed in the air, turning the
      modest flowers scarlet and loose
till the jonquils opened their throats and cackled out loud
when I broke my hand on her door and cried I was tortured
and she laughed and refused me, only one man in a crowd.

When I grew old, owning more than my share of the garden,
I loved a woman young and fresh as a larkspur trembling in the
      morning's translucent coolness,
her eyes had seen nothing but good, and as the sun's gold
rolled off her wrists with reluctance, she pardoned
my foolishness, laughed and turned me down gently, I was so old.

And when I fell ill, rooted in a damp house spotted with curses,
I loved a woman whose bones rustled like insect wings through the
      echoing darkening rooms
and the ceiling dropped like a gardener's hoe toward my bed
so I stretched out my hand to her begging my god for mercy
and she laughed and embraced me sweetly, I was so dead.

II. from Lines from Neuchâtel *(1974)*

Café du Pont

La vie est difficile, monsieur,
Madame Nicoud, our concierge,
said, mopping our kitchen floor
one afternoon. *Mais oui, vraiment*
I answered like a horse's ass
feeling stupid staring at my typewriter
while sweat poured over
Madame's square red face.
Her thick & battered legs bulged
as she knelt on the old tiles
prodding me to write something, anything.
So I type: *La vie est difficile, monsieur.*

~

I look out the window. Michel
is working in their small vineyard
on the sloping ground of Neuchâtel.
Across the lake the Alps are hid in mist,
the Alps are always hidden in the mist.
We know they're there.
Michel's wife left him for a captain
in the air force, an American. *Les américains
ont toujours beaucoup d'argent, m'sieu,*
he tells me. I try to look poor.
We *are* poor.
So why don't I work, *eh m'sieu?*

~

Swiss houses are turned backwards.
First you go through an iron gate
ten feet high with wicked spikes, then
walk around it, up steep steps
to the heavy entrance
facing a blank wall holding back
the foothills of the Jura Mountains.

Monsieur Nicoud keeps the steps immaculate,
picks up each leaf straying from the vine.
He'd like to catch them before they fall.
Except the Nicouds, Michel, & us,
nobody ever comes.

~

On Saturday night we all go out
together, along the narrow street
below the Suchard factory until, winding upward,
past the vineyards and the apple trees,
we see the tiles of the lower city
now black against the lake.
Bonsoir m'ssieurs 'dames: Jocelyn sings
her greetings at the door of the Café.
We eat, the food is good. We drink.
We drink to each other.
We drink to the Alps.
We know they're there.

Hôtel de la Truite

When we came up the Gorge that Sunday
John & Jeanne & I, the children running ahead
disappearing, appearing in the tall grass
we were dizzy from the rivercooled wine
so the hotel seemed at first a mirage:
we were in a movie, we were stars
the children's bounds turned suddenly slow motion
and silent, colors washed
pale as we held hands and approached
the tables under the ancient trees.
A painting by Seurat: Swiss families
clustered in the checkered shade, wine
bottles winked on colored tablecloths—
and then the sound turned on, Swiss music,
laughter, hands held out in welcome
glasses filled *pour les américains*
so we sat
at this crazy hotel in the woods
in the middle of beautiful nowhere
and almost forgot
the brooding darkness of America,
of all countries, the violence
of which we formed a part
and watched the children
under this neutral sky
John & Jeanne & I

Hôtel Lion d'Or

Taking the tram to Boudry was an adventure:
we could get off, along the way
at Auvernier, Colombier
little hamlets each with its café
some *spécialité* to set it off
and if one happened carelessly to cough
a little blood upon the tablecloth
why, in a minute it was whisked away.

Or we could get off between-towns, where the river
flicks shallow over stones, and in the shadows
speckled trout hang trembling, like leaves in air
and at the end, the old clock tower over Boudry
abandoned now, but lovely, and the clock of course
still working perfectly
this being Switzerland where life
ticks on correctly and the chimes
all come on cue. Thank you,
we *are* marvelous, and,
eating our escargots like good bourgeois
we sometimes shake our heads and forks to think
of poor Marat, bleeding in his bathtub,
born improbably in this very room
how many years ago?

Cabaret Voltaire

The fathers of all the pretty children
keep in the closet nearest the front door
a rifle oiled & waiting:
when the Russian wolf
leaps over the eastern Alps
boom   boom   boom
when the German dog
crosses the Bodensee
ouah   ouah   ouah
Switzerland will be ready
like a child doubling a fist
against his Daddy.

> *The swans of Lucerne swim round & round*
> *the tourists throw them pfennigs & pounds*
> *& the swans they gobble them down them down*
> *the swans they gobble them down*

O Switzerland where is your Dada now?
Where is your boomboomboom your
rosy Anna Blossom?
In the closet Dada's in the closet
where your little triggers fatten
like commas around a stiff proposition
where Freud forever sucks Napoleon's fingers
and there the lederhosen grin like clamshells
there the albino dwarf chewing on chicken bones
there the drain where Marat's blood
continually swirls, the closet never lies
like pretty girls, there pale parasites gnawing
something like money ouah ouah ouah
départ des trains suicides
boomboomboom
we follow where the red-eyed rabbits lead

Café Vue des Alpes

When the fog dropped swiftly
over the ski slope
all the pretty children
were lost among the trees.
Hallooo we cried Halloooo
but the fog swallowed our words
and hung them from the branches
pointing down, no human sound
could give direction there
and we stumbled blindly over
the treacherous snow, parents & children
lost and wandering
like leaves in a swirling pool.

The only sound
that somehow slipped the fog
and cut through thinly in irregular places
was music from some loudspeaker
or some café, a lively tune,
an accordion perhaps,
and slowly, in the fog, children & parents
began heading erratically toward the music
all of us separately, yet together
like leaves in a running stream;
at least we thought so,
being unable to see.

III. from The Night Train and
the Golden Bird *(1977)*

The Poet to His Tongue

The day they cut my tongue out
I spit a lot of blood but
basically was pleased:
I'd nothing to say, no one heard
and the damned thing was diseased anyway:
red-white cankerroses bloomed
words burned like houses
a sentence filled a room with dead birds

I don't believe in God
but I believe
God was trying to tell me something:
shut up.

Then, I took my tongue home
not wanting to lose it (him?) completely
and curled that infected rascal up
stuffed him in a bottle of Jim Beam
(which he favored when alive)
& stuck it on the windowsill
over my desk where I nightly
in silence nod to my ex-flesh
where it spins still, turning neat
as the moon
filters through dreams & whiskey
& sometimes strange music seems
to come from it, a strain
unnatural and familiar
that speaks of love and pain
& hope & pain
& pain & pain &

but maybe it comes from the beer joint across
the street

The Magic Kingdom

Why do so many fat people go to Disney World,
haunches lapping over the little seats
in the Grand Prix or Mr Toad's Wild Ride?
Does one feel weightless there, reality displaced
so you soon begin sniffing plastic roses
and they really smell like roses but better?

20,000 Leagues Under the Sea ("E" coupon)
we stare out our portholes at fake fish on wires,
the flat surface six inches above. Our kids ask,
Are the bubbles real?   Who knows?

The Master's dead: behold his Haunted House
at the top of Liberty Square (the orange map);
as Mickey said, he had a mind like a steel
mouse—and the smile of reason that
warmed the clean columns of Monticello
fades into the flat grin
of a mechanical Cheshire cat. Pink
pilgrims shoulder in the squares
cuddling the comic relics of infancy. In Fantasy-
land Mike Fink performs
an unnatural act on Dumbo the Unresisting
or is the heat getting me?

And yet
to stand in the middle of that circular movie
(admission free)
and see the crowd lean far to the left
feeling they're taking a curve
was (shall we say)
educational.

Chicken Unlimited

Today is our sixteenth anniversary
the suet anniversary, everything
turning to fat
At my side as I drive squats Chicken Unlimited
the sixteen-piece box: we have four kids
sometimes I think we eat too much chicken
it makes us want to kill each other

Our house is surrounded by oaks, azaleas
thriving on 6-6-6 and chicken bones
Chicken Unlimited is afraid of being alone, is
beautiful:
"scarlet circles ring your eyes
your bill as black as jet
like burnished gold your feathers gleam
your comb is devil red"
I think the sky is falling

Chicken Unlimited constantly breaks his neck
against an invisible shield
he can't get at the flowers

He is ambitious: wants to be president
wants to fuck the Queen
he wants to be Johnny Carson
he takes extension courses at night
but doesn't know what to think

I'm stuck in the traffic on 12th Street
the man behind honking like a crazed goose
I think he's after Chicken Unlimited
My son comes home bloody
"If I run, they call me chicken,
if I fight, he beats the shit out of me"

That's right, I say
that's the way it goes

Chicken Unlimited is jumping on my chest
its beak rakes my face
I think it wants to kiss me
I think it wants to eat me alive
I say, Chicken Unlimited
your kisses taste like wine
but I'm too old for this sort of thing

In the sky the constellations realign
the Big Dipper points to Chicken Unlimited
the rings of Saturn are grain
for its celestial gizzard
the sky is surely falling
One of my dreams is playing center field
in Yankee Stadium: C. U. is at bat,
smashes a towering drive I race back back
over the artificial grass
but the ball becomes an egg becomes
a bomb
as I/we crash together at the monument
Chicken Unlimited worries about his input
he wants to make it perfectly clear
but it still comes out cluckcluck
cluck cluck
he is weak on his relative pronouns

Daughter (age 9): Where do babies come from?
Mother: Why, from inside a woman.
D.: Yeah, how'd they get there?
M.: Well, let's see, how to explain it . . .
D.: Yeah, the old chicken in the bun, right?

Right.

Chicken Unlimited has such energy!
Like our kids
chicken tracks in the sooty snow
Still stuck in this insane traffic
man behind still honking me deaf
wanting to get home to my wife, my children
this crazy urge to stick my head
out the window, and yell
Compliments to the Chef!

(Untitled)

this is a poem to my son Peter
whom I have hurt a thousand times
whose large and vulnerable eyes
have glazed in pain at my ragings
thin wrists and fingers hung
boneless in despair, pale freckled back
bent in defeat, pillow soaked
by my failure to understand.
I have scarred through weakness
and impatience your frail confidence forever
because when I needed to strike
you were there to be hurt and because
I thought you knew
you were beautiful and fair
your bright eyes and hair
but now I see that no one knows that
about himself, but must be told
and retold until it takes hold
because I think anything can be killed
after a while, especially beauty
so I write this for life, for love, for
you, my oldest son Peter, age 10,
going on 11.

(Untitled)

You stand in isolation like the first bloom
of some enchanted plant. Around you lies a field
of sullen energy where strange creatures
only seen by you move in slow motion
with majestic beauty, their sharp hooves
spraying broken glass like water, the field
covered with the stained glass of old
cathedrals. And you are trapped in this magic
terrible land you more than half desire. I think
I hear you crying, I think you think
no one can reach you. Don't cry, look;
I'm taking off my shoes.
I'm coming in.

Third Child: June 11, 1962

Third child, it's crowded in my house
and heart. But here, I'll make a place
for you to lie, and sleep and cry.
Your world is crowded too: the mouse
is trapped, the kitten drowned, and dogs chase
dogs away, no place to stay,
no place to rest. The predatory
order of our days sharpens the claws
of children as they grow. I know
the center has not held, the glory
prophesied has died stillborn because
there was no room, there is no room . . .

No room for Gentile or for Jew;
East and West grapple in the dark
tied in one bag, cramming a flag
down one another's throats. And you,
third child, will seek in city parks
the room to run, but when the sun
sets it is not safe. You'll ask,
But why, why should I be afraid?
And I will say, Gretchen, the way
of man is dark, his face a mask
his outward life a grim charade
concealing narrow rooms, revealing
nothing. . . . Of course, I won't say that,
I'll say, Don't be afraid.
There's nothing to fear. I called you here
because it's bedtime, and that's that.
It's time you knelt beside your bed and prayed.

The Monkey's Paw

When the war is over the bones of the lonely dead
will knit and rise from ricefield and foxfield
like sea-things seeking the sea, and will head
toward their homes in Hanoi or Seattle
clogging the seaways, the airways, the highways
climbing the cliffs and trampling the clover
heading toward Helen, Hsueh-ying, or Mary
when the war is over

When the war is over Helen, Hsueh-ying, or Mary
and lonely women all over the world
will answer the knock on the door like that insane story
and find on their doorstep something they used to hold
in their arms, in their hearts, in their beds
and that something will reach out and crumble
and the eyes cave back in the head
when the war is over

When the war is over curses will mount in the air
like corbies, to flock over capital cities
and flutter and hover and waver and gather
till white buildings turn black beneath their cloud
and then they will drop like bombs, talons
zeroed in on the dead hearts still walking around
on the ground with memos in their briefcases
when the war, when the war is over

Ode to Good Men Fallen Before Hero Come

In all story before hero come
good men from all over set forth
to meet giant ogre dragon troll
and they are all killed every one
decapitated roasted cut in two
their maiden are carted away and gobbled like cupcake
until hero sail across white water
and run giant ogre dragon troll quite through

Land of course explode into rejoicing
and king's daughter kisses horny knight
but who's to kiss horny head of slaughtered
whose bony smile are for no one in particular
somewhere left out of story somebody's daughter
remain behind general celebration
combing her hair without looking into mirror
rethinking life without Harry who liked his beer

I sing for them   son friend brother
all women-born men like one we know
ourselves   no hero they no Tristan
no St. George Gawain Galahad Sgt. York
they march again and again to be quartered and diced
and what hell for them never attempt to riddle
I'm talking about Harry Smith caught in middle
who fought pretty bravely for nothing and screamed twice

Because

because
death is so lovely
so self-possessed
we have a tendency
to jump the gun
before the molecule's dissolution
the final bad breath

because
death is a communicable disease
only childless men
can commit suicide
without setting a time bomb
in the fragile cabins
of their children

and because
death is so attractive in the abstract
a rest
freedom from pain
we should bite our lips to remember
it doesn't taste good
it leaves a stain

The Heart's Location

all my plans for suicide are ridiculous
I can never remember the heart's location
too cheap to smash the car
too queasy to slash a wrist
once jumped off a bridge
almost scared myself to death
then spent two foggy weeks
waiting for new glasses

of course I really want to live
continuing my lifelong search
for the world's greatest unknown cheap restaurant
and a poem full of ordinary words
about simple things
in the inconsolable rhythms of the heart

Everything We Do

Everything we do is for our first loves
whom we have lost irrevocably
who have married insurance salesmen
and moved to Topeka
and never think of us at all.

We fly planes & design buildings
and write poems
that all say Sally I love you
I'll never love anyone else
Why didn't you know I was going to be a poet?

The walks to school, the kisses in the snow
gather as we dream backwards, sweetness with age:
our legs are young again, our voices
strong and happy, we're not afraid.
We don't know enough to be afraid.

And now
we hold (hidden, hopeless) the hope
that some day
she may fly in our plane
enter our building   read our poem

And that night, deep in her dream,
Sally, far in darkness, in Topeka,
with the salesman lying beside her,
will cry out
our unfamiliar name.

Surfaces

          darling
you are not at all
like a pool or a rose
my thoughts do not dart in your depths
like cool goldfish
nor does your skin suggest petals
you are not *like* anything (except perhaps
my idea of what you are like

I think you are like
what our children need to grow beautiful
what I need to be most myself)
when the moon comes out I do not think of you
but sometimes you remind me of the moon:
your surfaces are unbelievably real

This is how I feel about you:
suppose
on the surface of a rippling pool
the moon shone clearly reflected
like a yellow rose
then
if a cloud floated over it
          I would hate the sky

Elegy for a Diver

—for R. W.

I

Jackknife swandive gainer twist
high off the board you'd pierce the sky
& split the apple of the devil sun
& spit in the sun's fierce eye.
When you were young you never missed,
archer-diver who flew too high
so everything later became undone.

Later everything burned to ash
wings too close to the sun broke down
jackknife swandive gainer twist
can't be done on the ground
and nothing in your diver's past
had warned you that a diver drowns
when nothing replaces what is missed.

Everything beautiful falls away
jackknife swandive gainer twist
muscles drop and skin turns coarse
even skin the sun has kissed.
You drank the sun down every day
until the sun no longer existed
and only the drink had any force.

Only the drink had any force
archer-diver who flew too high
when you were young you never missed
& spit in the sun's fierce eye.

Later everything burned to ash:
everything beautiful falls away
even skin the sun has kissed
jackknife swandive gainer & twist

II

and now I see your bones in dreams
turning & twisting below our feet
fingerbones bending out like wings
as once again your body sings
swandiving slowly through the stone
that sparks your skull and shoulder bones
layer by layer and over and over
you flash through limestone sand & lava
feet together and backbone arched
like an arrow aimed at the devil's heart
the dead are watching your perfect dive
clicking their fingers as if alive
high off the board & the hell with the chances
once again your body dances
anything done well shines forever
only polished by death's dark weather
diver diver diving still
now & forever I praise your skill

Byron vs. Dimaggio

Yesterday I was told
the trouble with America is that
these kids here
would rather be DiMaggio
than Byron: this shows our decadence.
But I don't know,
there's not that much difference.
Byron also would have married Monroe
or at least been in there trying;
he too covered a lot of territory,
even with that bum foot,
and made the All-European swimming team
in the Hellespont League.

And, on the other hand, you
have to admit that DiMag played
sweet music
out there in the magic grass
of center field.

Teaching Poetry at a Country School
in Florida

It ain't there. Come off it, Rousseau.
The eyes roll inward, the brain coughs
like a motor at ten below

and doesn't start: they're not bad kids.
Too dumb for poetry, and smart enough to know
they don't need it: no one needs it:
not their teachers, nor principal, nor coach
who equates it with queers
and public masturbation
which unfortunately it sometimes resembles
particularly the iambic

But we have to do it because
in the midst of that tangible boredom—
from that stack of pathetic papers—
there is always one you come across
just before turning to drink
with thoughts of murder or suicide—
there is always one who writes
My wings are invisible but brilliant;
they carry me to the dark forest
where the unicorns kneel in prayer. . . .

So. You go on, after a while.
But still, all that effort, so little to show
like that royal palm outside my window going up & up
and up, with a small green *poof* at the top.

Plovers

—for Vaughn Morrison

How can a two-fingered poem catch a plover
in its feathers, piping the sandy beaches
over & over, scuttling stiff-legged skipping
in front of the ripple that rolls
                                     and reaches
for the quick feet always four inches
away? What can a poem say:
thick-billed, black-bellied, killdeer, turnstone,
words rolling in front of the wave
or clicking tiptoe across black rocks
like a flock of birds.

Hartley hunted plovers all his life
catching them on canvas one by one—
black-bellied killdeer thick-billed & turnstone—
all kinds, painting them standing, nesting, marching,
hopping, writing poems about them on the back
of his paintings; all kinds, but always hunting
for that rare golden plover that never appeared,
never whistled down the long stretches of shore
from Maine to North Carolina, the bird
that all of God's bird-watchers dream about.

Some day a poem of mine snapping across the
white reaches of blank space just ahead of the
blind sea in which all is lost may swing
around the bend clickety-clack and find
chuckling unaware that golden plover O rare
shining in glorious sunlight unafraid
around its neck a silver clasp with a poem
of Hartley's rolled inside head & back erect
on long quick legs and will run around
over & through it eyes wings beak will be mine

the poem will cradle that bird & protect
and caress those unbelievable soft feathers & frail bone
and will take it all alone to Cape Cod
or Narragansett an abandoned beach
on a rainy day by the cold sea
and there I suppose
will give it back to Hartley & it will be
a feather in the golden cap of God

Dear Reader

Why don't you write you never
write   each day I check the mail
nothing but truss ads & christmas seals
where are you what are you doing
tonight?

How are your teeth?
When I brush mine blood
drips down my chin
are you happy do you miss me
I will tell you
there is no one like you
your eyes are unbelievable
your secrets are more interesting than anyone else's
you had an unhappy childhood
right?

I will rub your feet they're tired
I'll say Hey
let's go to the movies
just the 2 of us
love

peter

IV. from Trying to Surprise God *(1981)*

Supermarket

My supermarket is bigger than your supermarket. That's
what America's all about. Nowhere am I happier,
nowhere am I more myself. In the supermarket, there
you feel free. Listen: the carts roll
on their oiled wheels, the cash register sings
to the Sound of Music, the bag boys are unbearably polite!
Everywhere there are lies, but in the supermarket we speak truth.
The sallow young man by the cornstarch bumps my cart,
I tell him, There are always two brothers. One is
hardworking, serious. The other is good looking but worthless;
he drinks, he is a natural athlete, he seduces Priscilla
Warren whom the older brother loves, and then abandons her.
Yes, cries the sallow young man, O my god yes!
Everywhere there are lies, I lie to my classes, I say,
Eat this poem. Eat that poem. *Good* for you.
I say, Sonnets have more vitamins than villanelles,
I give green stamps for the most vivid images.
But in the supermarket truth blows you over like a clearance sale.
I meet Mrs. Pepitone by the frozen fish, dark circles
under her dark eyes. I tell her, If we had met 16 years earlier
in the dairy section perhaps, everything would have been different.
Yes! Mrs. Pepitone cracks a Morton pie in her bare hands, lust
floods the aisles, a tidal wave, everyone staring
at everyone else with total abandon; Mr. Karakis is streaking
through the cold cuts! Outside, the lies continue.
We lie in church, we say
Buy Jesus and you get Mary free. If you have faith
you can eat pork, dollar a chop.
We give plaid stamps for the purest souls.
I meet Sue Morgan by the family-sized maxi-pads. Or
is it mini-pads?—Or is it mopeds? In the supermarket
everything sounds like everything else. I tell her,
You can see azaleas even in the dark, the white ones
glow like the eyes of angels. I tell her, Azaleas
are the soul of the South, you kill all azaleas

Jimmy Carter will shrivel like a truffle. Yes,
she exclaims, Hallelujah! And still the lies
pile up on the sidewalk, they're storming
the automatic doors. Mr. Hanratty the manager throws himself
in front of the electronic beam, he knows this means
he will be sterile forever, but the store comes first:
the lies retreat to the First National Bank
where they meet no resistance. Meanwhile,
in the supermarket I am praising truth-in-advertising
laws, I am trying to figure the exact price per ounce,
the precise percentage of calcium propionate. And
for you, my tenderest darling, to whom I always return
laden with groceries, I bring Spaghetti-O's and chocolate
kisses, I tip whole shelves into my cart, the bag boys
turn pale at my approach, they do isometric exercises.
But I know this excess is unnecessary,
I say, My friends, think Small, use the 8-item line, who
needs more than 8 items? All you really need is
civility, honesty, courage, and 5 loaves of wheatberry bread.
Listen friends, Life is no rip-off, the oranges are full of
juice, their coloring the best we can do, why do you think
we live so long?   So long.

My dear friends, the supermarket is open. Let us begin.

Robert Frost in Warsaw

When I saw birches in Wasienki Park
leaning against the wind, I thought of you,
old ghost, so strongly have you claimed those trees
for us. Even here, four thousand miles away
from Derry or Franconia, your voice,
through foreign though familiar leaves, whispers
that the human heart can neither forfeit
nor accept responsibilities. Even
here, where storms far wilder, blacker, than those
which strike New Hampshire have torn up the stones
and thrown uncounted populations
into hells we only read about, your poems
proclaim ambiguous affirmation
in the dark. I sit here in a rented room
with you, heart pumping as I read your lines,
and think of parents, wife, and children
who travel with me complicated roads
beneath a winter sky that hides the stars.
They tell me you were selfish: it may be so.
I know you spoke to me through birches in
Wasienki Park, kindly, and brought me home.

Azaleas

In the morning, in December
they lean like flares over our brick pathway,
vessels of fragrant energy,
their bright explosions enclosed by the frailest membrane:
they tremble with their holy repressions.
We watch; we tremble, too. We learn.

They thrive on acid, these azaleas; they burn
in darkness, loving the shadows of old oaks
whose broken leaves flutter down to feed
their flowering fantasies.

For surely azaleas are not real, they grow
in some deep wilderness of soul, some known
ideal of vulnerability made palpable,
whose thin petals float dying to the ground
even as we walk by, without touching.
Our very presence seems to kill.

We know more than we can say: we live
in waves of feelings and awareness
where images unfold and grow
along the leafwork of our nerves and veins;
and when one morning late in March
we walk out on our porch and see
the white azaleas open to the air
we recognize them from our dreams
as every cell projects our affirmation.

O Pride of Mobile, Maiden Blush,
Prince of Orange, President Clay:
the names are humorous examples
of human hubris—O Glory of Sunninghill!
And yet they're touching, too: my salmon-
colored Duc de Rohan's fragile aristocracy

doomed like his forebears to lose his head;
your Elegans, that early bloomer,
whose petals lie like butterflies on our walk
or pastel Kleenex thickly strewn
in some orgy of melancholy weeping. . . .

Dwarves and Giants, Pinkshell, Flame—
O my dear, so many azaleas are dying!
We must have a party! Here! This afternoon!

Ping-Pong

Outside, the children play Ping-Pong
beneath the trees. Click-clock click-clock
the ball ticks back & forth through
shadow and leaflight, paddles flash
red and green, red
and green to the eternal
amazement of squirrels in the branches
of field mice in the scattered woodpile

Inside, the halls are ankle deep in blood
the mother hunches in the closet the
father rages through the house breaking mirrors.
Behind the refrigerator the mouse
with broken neck testifies to the reality
of the situation: There is something wrong it
is no one's fault. Roaches drop in saucers
the spider spins with total concentration

This is not a moment this is forever.
Tomorrow, the children will play Ping-Pong
beneath the trees, the mother's eyes open
to betrayal the father's fist clenched
in disappointment the blood rolling across
the floor wave on wave forever
while the ball spins through shadow & light
to the unchanging cries of bright-eyed children

World Within World

I

World within world, like Chinese boxes
the sameness of everything fills one with awe:
rabbits are hunted by people and foxes
and foxes are hunted by dogs with their people
and people are hunted like dogs by the people
who clutch in their foxholes a rabbit's dead paw.

World within world, the shore and the ocean
are made like our bodies of drops and grains
and the earth is a grain in the ocean of sky
and the sky is a drop in the bloodstream of God
and the drops in our bloodstreams are moved by the motion
that moves all the rivers that run in God's brain.

II

And even you, who I think perhaps
hold in your veins the impossible
93rd element, even your eyes
as quick as foxes, the whiteness
of your hand: so many drops
of water; so many grains of sand.

The Death of the Pilot Whales

Every few years, down at the Florida Keys,
where bones chew the water like mad dogs
and spit it bubbling out on yellow sand,
the sea darkens, and we crane toward the skies,
toward the airplanes casting their shadows,
but there are no planes and those dark shadows
are not shadows, but mark the silent forms
of pilot whales charging the shore like wild
buffalo charging a train, driving toward
reef and sand till the foam sprays red
below the rainbow stretching from sea to land.

The fierceness of it all, unstoppable,
those broad flukes churning the water, that buried
brain and heart set inflexibly on their last
pulsing, the energy and beauty of all that
flesh turning away from its cold fathomless
world, like the negative of some huge
lemming following god knows whose orders
in a last ordered chaos of frantic obedience
stronger than love. With what joy and
trembling they hunch up the beach,
shred themselves on shoals, what sexual
shudders convulse them at that sweet moment
when they reach—at last!—what
they have burned to meet.

And we, who may be reminded of thoughts
we wish not to think, we tow them back to sea,
cut them open, and they sink.

from "Lines from Key West"

I. Hero Worship at Key West on the 4th of July

The midget in Sloppy Joe's
had a wooden leg: you said
They don't even make midgets like they used to:
Papa would've used that leg
to stir his drink with.
Drunk, I later slipped on the rocks
and lay on my back in the water
watching the fireworks.
All around there were midgets
watching the fireworks,
their high voices rising like birds
in the darkness. Really, they said, and
Really

II. Writing the Great American Poem in Key West

I always believed, he said, the examined life
isn't worth living: all those pores & betrayals,
betrayals & pores. He smoothed the tablecloth;
he looked around. *Mother,* he wrote. *Father.*
And the room became still. The customers cried
in their beer, the bartender cried
saying, You have seen through us,
every one.
        But the tablecloth, that
you'll have to pay for.

III. Playing Shuffleboard, Drunk, in Key West, Fla.

So quiet. Even the dogs
were pussyfooting around
under the lights of the shuffleboard court.
Clok went the discs as the critic knocked
the poet out of the "7" box. What
is a breath, the critic asked,
but a weaving of words on the night air's loom?
I don't give a shit, the poet replied.
Don't crowd me.
Give me room.

VIII. Wishing He Had a Theory in Key West

He wanted to have a theory, all
great poets have theories, even
though they're nuts (the theories, that is):
Yeats's gyres, Pound's money,
Williams's triads, Olson's
breath, Bly's deep images, and acres of poets
turning Catholic or renouncing Catholicism,
what fun to be so sure of oneself, what fun
recanting one's previous surenesses. And
writing poems about all of this, that
was the point, the poems spill out from
theories, pure peas from piddling pods.

His theory was, to have a theory
you need mainly hunger & meanness
which live on theories
like snakes on mice

but what could he do
in this generous sleepy town
at the end of the world
and him a vegetarian besides?

The Poet, Trying to Surprise God

The poet, trying to surprise his God
composed new forms from secret harmonies,
tore from his fiery vision galaxies
of unrelated shapes, both even & odd.
But God just smiled, and gave his know-all nod
saying, "There's no surprising One who sees
the acorn, root, and branch of centuries;
I swallow all things up, like Aaron's rod.

So hold this thought beneath your poet-bonnet:
no matter how free-seeming flows your sample
God is by definition the Unsurprised."
"Then I'll return," the poet sighed, "to sonnets
of which this is a rather pale example."

"Is that right?" said God. "I hadn't realized. . . ."

In Gentler Times

In gentler times, if times were ever gentle,
you'd blossom in a peasant blouse and dirndl
to linger by a stream below a windmill
while I would weave, upon my poet's spindle,
bright cloth for your white shoulders, a gold mantle
of shining praise to cover love's old temple;
but now, my love, we know no such example
of hopeful days, if hope were ever ample.

Today, hope stutters like a guttering candle,
the dark too dark for love alone to handle;
Godot, because unknown, is worse than Grendel,
and love uncertain seems a certain swindle.

And yet my love, our love's as quick to kindle
as simpler loves, if love were ever simple.

Sonnet on the Death of the Man Who Invented Plastic Roses

The man who invented the plastic rose
is dead. Behold his mark:
his undying flawless blossoms never close
but guard his grave unbending through the dark.
He understood neither beauty nor flowers,
which catch our hearts in nets as soft as sky
and bind us with a thread of fragile hours:
flowers are beautiful because they die.

Beauty without the perishable pulse
is dry and sterile, an abandoned stage
with false forests. But the results
support this man's invention; he knew his age:
a vision of our tearless time discloses
artificial men sniffing plastic roses.

Mendel's Laws

I

A monk can do his work on bended knees
inside or out; the bishop looked askance
when Mendel labored in a row of peas
and led the combinations in their dance.
The spark of genius dominates the heavens
and sparkles in the furrow and the loam;
both earth and sky are broken down in sevens
and Christ is captured in a chromosome.

My lover, this was many years ago.
Mendel became abbot and then died.
But all his scorned experiments proved so:
the row of peas spoke truth, the bishop lied.
And what has this to do with us? I'm wild
to know it all since you are now with child.

II

The double helix and the triple star
work in conjunction, like harmonic tones,
and I will praise—how beautiful you are!—
the spiral staircase turning through your bones.
Genetic links, for better and for worse,
bind us to all creation: in my ears
your voice has blended with the universe
and vibrates with the music of the spheres.

Your fingers on the keys at Christmastide,
so effortless in their precise selection,

pick out the ancient chords; while I, beside
you, turn the pages at each soft direction
and wonder at your slender hands because
your fingers follow God's and Mendel's laws.

III

When Eve was cloned from Adam's rib, and stood
by the serpent underneath the Tree
she understood what lovers understood
since first they separated from the sea.
Her choice was meagre; still, she had to choose;
and we, like Eve, have chosen ever since,
face to face, the brown eyes to the blues:
it is the choosing makes the difference.

And in the code that Mendel labored on
our child will be deciphered; there will merge,
in childish shape and spirit, a paragon
where paradox and paradigm converge.
Now I can see Eve's children in your eyes:
completely new, yet linked to paradise.

Myrtle the Turtle

MYRTLE THE TURTLE   P.S. 222

. because we always said Toity-toid Street and
Shut da daw Miss Endicott devised an exercise
for us so we could lose our accent and become
president of the united states . but Bobby
Pepitone said Shit he din wanna be no president
y'ever see a president chewin gum? nosir . but
we had to do the exercise anyway it was a poem
called Myrtle the Turtle . we were supposed to
recite very clearly There once was a *turtle*
whose *first* name was *Myrtle* swam out to the
Jersey shore but of course we each got up in
front of the class scratching ourselves and
ducking spitballs and said Aah dere once wuz
a toitle whose foist name wuz Moitle while Miss
Endicott tore her hair out . I just visited
Bobby Pepitone and to judge by the way his kids
talk poor Miss Endicott must be completely bald
by now . like a toitle his kids would say .

Helen

A mad sculptor in our park
has fashioned there, in writing bronze,
the old story of Leda and the swan.
There, the trees are cool and dark
and men may sit and contemplate
the myriad forms that love can take.

And on the cement pedestal, between
the burning figures and the cool grass,
is scrawled in printing recognizably obscene,
Helen Goldberg is a good peece of ass.

Ah, Helen Goldberg, your mortal lover
has proved false, and, what is worse,
illiterate. Tell me, did he hover
swanlike above your trembling skirts
in a burst of light and shadow,
or were you surprised by a shower
of gold, shining like El Dorado
in your surrendering hour?

But probably you shifted your gum from one side
to the other while he had trouble
with his skin-tight pants (not yours)
and you hoped later he'd give you a ride
on his cycle—and anyway love's a bubble
that bursts like gum in feminine jaws.

There should be a moral here, and yet
I'd be willing to bet
there was no swan back then, either,
just a story that brown-haired Leda
made up for her mother to explain
why she was late again,
and her lovely daughter didn't hatch from an egg,

but was born in the same inelegant way
as Helen Goldberg, whose pointed breasts
and bottom-twitching walk
devastated all of 77th Street West,
Troy 23, New York.

To a Daughter with Artistic Talent

—for Perrie

I know why, getting up in the cold dawn
you paint cold yellow houses
and silver trees. Look at those green birds,
almost real, and that lonely child looking
at those houses and trees.
You paint (the best way) without reasoning,
to see what you feel, and green birds
are what a child sees.

Some gifts are not given: you
are delivered to them,
bound by chains of nerves and genes
stronger than iron or steel, although
unseen. You have painted every day
for as long as I can remember
and will be painting still
when you read this, some cold
and distant December when the child
is old and the trees no longer silver
but black fingers scratching a gray sky.

And you never know why (I was lying
before when I said I knew).
You never know the force that drives you wild
to paint that sky, those birds flying,
and is never satisfied today
but maybe tomorrow
when the sky is a surreal sea
in which you drown . . .

I tell you this with love and pride
and sorrow, my artist child
(while the birds change from green to blue to brown).

Advice to My Son

—for Tim

The trick is, to live your days
as if each one may be your last
(for they go fast, and young men lose their lives
in strange and unimaginable ways)
but at the same time, plan long range
(for they go slow: if you survive
the shattered windshield and the bursting shell
you will arrive
at our approximation here below
of heaven or hell).

To be specific, between the peony and the rose
plant squash and spinach, turnips and tomatoes;
beauty is nectar
and nectar, in a desert, saves—
but the stomach craves stronger sustenance
than the honied vine.
Therefore, marry a pretty girl
after seeing her mother;
speak truth to one man,
work with another;
and always serve bread with your wine.

But, son,
always serve wine.

V. from Underneath the Lantern *(1986)*

Flatbush

*Ach, wen vermögen
wir denn zu brauchen?*

—Rilke, "The First Elegy"

Where Nostrand crosses Flatlands Avenue
there are no Sisters of the Sacred Well
nor are we harps of inspiration
on which the heavenly winds make holy song.
And yet the voices of my vanished aunts
blow in from somewhere, and they say
(with Brooklyn accent, each in her own way):

*The world, unfairly fair, is a tall home
among many, and there is not a nail
or dish or key whose history does not
contain such multitudes of mystery
we could not count them, even if we dared.
Like the bow and arrow who loved each other
we send you out, free in a different world,
to land in your own place but speak of ours.
Tell them how we suffered, how we cried.*

(All except me! each archer, smiling, lied. . . .)

89

The House

Let us say there is an ideal realm
whose spires and minarets send endless light
above white avenues of pine and elm.
Below this, or inside, the real world
shifts its shoulders in its struggle
to be born, to grow toward possibility.
Cities flash and shudder in the sun, whole forests
disappear beneath the blade, and everywhere
some inchling of a tree is pushing
its pale question, some family plants and hammers
in the shadow of a slanting roof.
In the middle of this second world,
near Flatlands Avenue in Brooklyn,
my father and grandfather bought
with banging hearts and hesitant hands
and miniscule down payment, a skinny,
dark, three-storied house, brick stoop
in front, small yard in back;
and through its heavy door our vivid aunts
and uncles thrust their demanding way
in a tumbling stream of family and friends,
dogs, cats, parakeets, and turtle. Unlike
the condominium of today—now
towering in its place—this was a house
that could be called a house, passionate
and painful, splintered forever in this mix
of orbiting atoms, mortar and memory,
story, stone, and blood.

Uncle Jim

What the children remember about Uncle Jim
is that on the train to Reno to get divorced
so he could marry again
he met another woman and woke up in California.
It took him seven years to untangle that dream
but a man who could sing like Uncle Jim
was bound to get in scrapes now and then:
he expected it and we expected it.

Mother said, It's because he was the middle child,
and Father said, Yeah, where there's trouble
Jim's in the middle.

When he lost his voice he lost all of it
to the surgeon's knife and refused the voice box
they wanted to insert. In fact he refused
almost everything. *Look,* they said,
*it's up to you. How many years
do you want to live?* and Uncle Jim
held up one finger.
The middle one.

Stille Nacht, Heilege Nacht

At Christmas, my sisters and I
learned to sing carols in German:
Grandpa would give us a quarter
apiece for performing, though
only Carol could carry a tune.
After the start of the War
Father forbade us to practice,
and when Grandpa asked for his songs
we told him they weren't allowed.
You are German, he shouted. Sing!

Singt, meine kinder, für mich!

We stood mute, unhappy, ashamed,
between father and son locking eyes
while the U-boats were nosing the currents
and propellers coughed in the skies
like angels clearing their throats.

Uncle Joe

Let a fool throw a stone into a well,
said Uncle Joe, and ten wise men
can't get it up again. I said, Put
Carol in a bucket and *she* could get it,
and Melinda said, Who'd want it anyway?
and Mother said, You're not putting Carol
into any bucket and Uncle Jim said,
Those wise men never seem to get it up.

Uncle Joe motioned for another manhattan.
One chops the wood, he said,
the others do the grunting.

Aunt Mary

In the dining room against the wall
a patient upright Kimball, painted black,
waited for the children's painful lessons
to be over, for evening when the sisters sang.
Aunt Mary, who was fat and never married,
had perfect pitch, and she could play by ear
any song, in any key, you could hum or whistle.
But she returned always to the old ones:
Lili Marlene, Cockles and Mussels, The Riddle,
Muss i Denn.

         Often, up too late,
we children knelt at our bedroom window
while their voices sifted through the gauze
curtains onto the shadowed Brooklyn street,
and watched the walkers suddenly slow
their feet, pause for a moment at the strains
of "Underneath the lantern / By the barrack gate . . ."
the longing in those voices taking root
and blossoming in us all like a tree
of knowledge untranslatable and true.

Aunt Gertrud

My seven aunts never left Brooklyn,
but Aunt Gertrud read travel books so hard
she felt she actually had gone.
The fish in Macedonia, she'd say,
you vouldn't belief—they melt in your mouth
like cream cheese! And never, she warned her sisters,
their gray heads bobbing like barn owls,
never stand alone on a corner in Naples!

Her travels made her liberal, and when
some other aunt would lecture
about our ungodly hours, she'd stroke
my surly head and say, eyes round as rupees—

Vell,
you're vunce only young, ain't it?

The Cloud, Florida, 1985

Above mimosa and the flowering palm,
above the lights that narrow to a V,
beyond the streaming headlights, past the lake,
beyond the skyline biting at the sky,
below the lonely star pegged near a cloud
like a penny nail holding the whole thing up,
this cloud, solid as iron, chunky as coal,
squats like a Buddha on the pale horizon.
Clouds are Florida's mountains, palpable
as stone with snowy tufts, or dizzying
stadiums of sound and light. They
satisfy the heart by filling emptiness
with shape—but this one I have seen before. . . .

Underneath the lantern. My hands tighten
on the wheel. Not like a Buddha now but still
triangular, slabs of dust and gas layered
like steps, a boy could run right up or tumble
down. . . .
        Slowly, the coalescing clouds
sharpen like snapshots in the darkening sky,
lit from below by the departed sun;
and I know the shape: the side view of
our house in Flatbush, even the right color—
slate blue-gray. *It is burning, burning!*
and I stop the car to watch as the light flares
one last time and the shape blurs and fades
into the broken air, racing always
farther away from Brooklyn, toward the last
borough where all their voices sleep.

VI. from Night Watch on the Chesapeake
(1987)

.

Night Watch on the Chesapeake

—for Paul Van Dongen

The North Star beams us cleanly down the Patuxent
into the waiting mouth of Chesapeake Bay,
past Sandgate on starboard, Sollers on port,
with a crescent moon rocking us toward day.
In the engine room there are fifteen dials to watch;
I check their stories every twenty minutes
—earplugs deadening the engine's hungry roar—
noting them down in the log: oil pressure in #2
reads a little high: call the pilot house
to back it off a hundred RPM. . . .

                                   I too am waiting.

After Point Patience I stare hard through the darkness,
my eyes knowing where it is, the years
sinking like ships through the watery moonlight. . . .

And there is the spire I have watched for,
deep in the Solomons, whiter than scallop flesh,
slim as the bones of my brother who went with me
to Our Lady Star of the Sea and loved
Sister Margaret and pulled the blueclaws up
with infinite gentleness on chicken necks tied to a string,
who now rests somewhere in the complex currents
off Point Patience where the pirates used to circle
waiting for tides. The good Sister taught us
poetry and my brother never sailed
without his salt-stiff copy of Shelley or Blake
which he'd read to the fish and the stubborn crab
and made his life as rich as any of God's lost children
could ever hope for, so I finish my coffee,
replacing it with whiskey, wishing it were wine,
and raise my cup in the stern starlight, toasting
Sister Margaret with all her sixth-grade sailors

whom she cannot save, but will comfort through
the cold night watches while they try to decipher
the spinning dials and luminescent whispers of the ship's long wake.

A Church Cemetery in St. Mary's

Across the landing strip, past planes
with folded wings sleeping like beetles
grown gargantuan in a summer's dream,
the runner turns inland, plunging
into shade and overgrowth where Indian
and pilgrim wrestled to a foregone conclusion
and the Susquehannocks and all their kin
were terminated with extreme prejudice,
as we have learned to say. Today
all that is left are names—Piscataway,
Patuxent, Chaptico, Mattapany—but
the heavy scent of honeysuckle
and mountain laurel, wild cherry
and wild rose, shows him that nature makes
the best of death: rabbits run
in playful figure eights
before him on the path, quail zip
about like Keystone Kops, while fawns
peer from the shadows fringing
the small church cemetery he bursts upon.

The smallness of it, that's what touches him.
The leaning markers and the fading dates
are picturesque, but in his life
he has run far and seen the graves
in Warsaw and Verdun and Arlington,
whole countrysides abandoned
to this stacking up of corpses side by side.
How manageable we used to be—
a runner can get his mind around
a cemetery scaled like this. . . .
                              (But now,
his turn on watch, he turns around,
heading for the naval base, his
silent neighborhood of transients

where no one picks up hitchhikers;
when the path goes from gravel into tar
he pads past streets named Shepard, Schirra,
Chaffee, the convex Testing Centers
marked "Off Limits," even for him,
and wonders exactly what is tested
in these forbidden structures, so near
the old church graveyard in St. Mary's.

Rage

Eighteen below: the black-capped chickadee
bangs on the suet in front of the cat
pressing against the pane. The woodpile
sprawls below the porch, the woodsmoke shadow
solid as the snow, the emptiness
where the old elm used to be—all frozen forever
in this scene, by these words, on this page:
a poor farmhouse broken down by age.

And rage, too, will never go away, never;
your disappointment, bitter as ash, more
murderous than this weather,
is part of what we'd taste like now
if whatever's in the woods got in the house.
You're sleeping now: you never had it better.

The Slow Child

The slow child kneels before the burning leaves,
his pupils denser than the tree's dark trunk,
his laces lolling limp as worms, hands
hung loosely in the scented air
where electric bluejays cock their clever heads
teasing the cat that tenses in the weeds.

The languid monarchs open, close, their wings
as if no enemy were near;
the boy is natural as a stump:
though neither blind nor deaf
he holds his body steady while
all lively things around him fight for breath.

The odor of red tide seeps inland when
the grouper and the jack turn belly-up,
and meets the puff of phosphate in a mix
as civilized as dollar bills. Combustion
motors cough along the lane where houses
eat the shoreline and taxes go for guns.

Unmoved,
unmoving,
unblinking eye of two hearts' hurricane,
you squat, dead center, on the lawn.
God-touched child, Edenic pool,
flower purer than the clinging rose—

from your unharming mind no acid flows,
and all your alabaster hands create
is something that resembles love's estate
and curls like incense through the darkened house,
twisting in attic shadow where the mouse
stares with dumb gratitude at the poisoned bait.

Blue Morning Glories

The oak trees lean their elbows on
our upstairs porch: that's bow the boys
get in. Blue morning glories run
around the trunks: the noise

of lizard, squirrel, oriole,
and jay. Everything seems simple:
the sun pulls like a pump, it pulls
water through the oak, the tendril

of the vine around the trunk.
Chloroplasts pace like prisoners
around the crowded cells, they drink
deep draughts of water, light, and air.

The body knows what it needs
to stay alive, water or whiskey;
the hearts of oaks and roses bleed
like ours; still, they work precisely:

they can measure day;
they know when to flower.
Darling, why should only they
control the hour?

Our timing's always off:
at the particular minute
one always hears a cough,
one's heart's not in it.

To live a single day
like a flower or oak
would make my body sway
till my heart broke

for all we might have done,
for me, for you—
something simple, like sun
on blue.

Atomic Pantoum

In a chain reaction
the neutrons released
split other nuclei
which release more neutrons

The neutrons released
blow open some others
which release more neutrons
and start this all over

Blow open some others
and choirs will crumble
and start this all over
with eyes burned to ashes

And choirs will crumble
the fish catch on fire
with eyes burned to ashes
in a chain reaction

The fish catch on fire
because the sun's force
in a chain reaction
has blazed in our minds

Because the sun's force
with plutonium trigger
has blazed in our minds
we are dying to use it

With plutonium trigger
curled and tightened
we are dying to use it
torching our enemies

Curled and tightened
blind to the end
torching our enemies
we sing to Jesus

Blind to the end
split up like nuclei
we sing to Jesus
in a chain reaction

Hermann Ludwig Ferdinand Von Helmholtz

Hermann Helmholtz said the problem facing
the scientist is this:
reduce a creek, a kiss,
a flaming coal from this random tracing

to some irreducible final text
dancing to the air
of the inverse square,
and we are left with the question: what next?

But there is always another layer
above, beyond, below
the last answer: we know
the scientist and poet shape their prayer

with Newton and Frost, who searched for order
instead of answers and found
such grace in number and sound
they glorify the spell of light on water.

Running with the Hyenas

—for Allen Joyce

At 5:00 A.M., in silence, song,
you coast through half-remembered notes,
high, low, white, and black: nightsnow molding
the burrowed city. Though it falls zero
or below, you feel nothing, layered
in old clothes, Vaseline over forehead and nose.
Yours the first steps on the crust, hiss and whisper,
flakes swirl in shallow lamplight, ice thickens
on your whitening beard and the Pleiades
cluster in your chest. You
run, dizzy from childhood, crying with happiness:
First out! First out! But where's your sister,
to make angels in the snow? Now, circling
the park, you wind through the zoo and all sleep,
the lion, white tiger, one-humped dromedary,
where is your father, to name you the names, what
is that shape and whose laughter? Where
is your mother now, so far, so deep?

And suddenly you are not alone: on your left
something is awake, keeping pace in the darkness.
Bodies smudged against snow, across
the moat, they lope grunting beside you so
you turn, and they turn and stay with you,
a grown man, over and over, back and forth
in the zoo; and not for love.

The ABC of Aerobics

Air seeps through alleys and our diaphragms
balloon blackly with this mix of
carbon monoxide and the thousand corrosives a city
doles out free to its constituents;
everyone's jogging through Edgemont Park,
frightened by death and fatty tissue,
gasping at the maximal heart rate,
hoping to outlive all the others streaming
in the lanes like lemmings lurching toward their last
jump. I join in despair
knowing my arteries jammed with
lint and tobacco, lard and bourbon—my
medical history a noxious marsh:
newts and moles slink through the sodden veins,
owls hoot in the lungs' dark branches;
probably I shall keel off the john like
queer Uncle George and lie on the bathroom floor
raging about Shirley Clark, my true love in
seventh grade, God bless her wherever she lives
tied to that turkey who hugely
undervalues the beauty of her tiny earlobes, one
view of which (either one: they are both perfect)
would add years to my life, and I could skip these
X-rays, turn in my insurance card, and trade
yoga and treadmills and jogging and zen and
zucchini for drinking and dreaming of her, breathing hard.

The Gift of the Magi

The angel of the Lord sang low
and shucked his golden slippers off
and stretched his wings as if to show
their starlit shadow on the wall
and did the old soft shoe, yeah,
did the buck and wing.

The Magi put their arms around
each other, then with chorus line
precision and enormous zest
they kicked for Jesus onetwothree
high as any Christmas tree
and Caspar was the best.

And Melchior told a story that
had Joseph sighing in the hay
while holy Mary rolled her eyes
and Jesus smiling where he lay
as if he understood, Lord,
knew the joke was good.

But Balthazar began to weep
foreseeing all the scenes to come:
the Child upon a darker stage
the star, their spotlight, stuttering out—
then shook his head, smiled, and sang
louder than before.

There was no dignity that night:
the shepherds slapped their sheepish knees
and tasted too much of the grape
that solaces our sober earth
O blessèd be our mirth, hey!
Blessèd be our mirth!

Vision

—for Carol

Sometimes, though the sun is high,
the Catskills lie invisible in mist
and only the veined and dripping maple leaf
near your window focuses in a burst of green.
Some days the fog sinks or rises like a magic carpet
and we see the disembodied peaks
or cut-off valley so the world is textured
in extremes. Barrel-hard, deer-soft,
ice and angelhair float before us,
an illustrated lecture claiming vision's a gift
fleeting and arbitrary as love.

You can feel the rough boards of the room
with their smooth knotholes and know it's pine,
this is what pine feels like, brittle and dry.
Glass feels wet, stones dense as lead. You search the fabric
of your chair for the ridged seam, the loose thread.
All things have tongues that call into your curved
and outspread fingers, even colors seem to whisper
in the dark. Blue, says the sofa, and your fingers hear.

No one has such hands: your heliotropic
children blossom from their blessing, turning
as you circle on familiar rounds to touch your world
lightly as the sun glances off calico
or the Hudson River bending out of sight.
You must think we all look younger than we are,
frozen in the year the nerve ends died
and sight diminished as by rheostat
or stage light fading in the final act.
That was when I still could play baseball
and you could catch, squatting on calloused heels
wiggling the too-big glove, crying OK, turkey,
zing it hard as you can!

113

Now lines and shadows touch us all, the sockets
sinking, cheekbones pushing up in the family way,
as if the skull were shouting, Here I am!
I think you've missed little, memory's kinder
than the eye. And the new movies, the new books—
not for us. Old Rip Van Winkle, weathering
with his gun, saw nothing worth reporting
those twenty years: he knew what he knew.
My vision's 20/20, yet to me
you still have freckles and your red hair flares
like unexpected silence in the sun.

Fourth of July

The stars were brighter than the fireworks
that night, as if the mountains held a cup
of water and they floated on the surface
right above them, drowning in the valley.
Look, she said, the fireflies are just as big
as stars. *Come back,* he said. *I can't hear
anyone but you. Can't make myself pay attention.*
Did you collect them when you were a boy? she
asked. *Yes.* Punch holes in lids of mason jars
with ice picks? *Yes.* Did you put grass in there
so they wouldn't be afraid? *No,* he said.
*At least, I don't remember. I need to tell you
I'm incomplete when you're not with me.*
You should have put grass in there, she said.
That was important. The fireworks were crackling
to an end, long streamers curving down the cheek
of night. Now he could see the Archer, aiming
north, the only constellation
he could name in all that vast
bewilderment of light.

Fifty on Fifty

On my fiftieth birthday I shall give up symbols:
no more pools or tunnels, it's flat statements
from now on. What good is being fifty
if you can't loosen your belt and be disgusting?
The world is blessed by beautiful women,
I will cry. *Which is not lovely at 9 P.M.?*
A fair number, perhaps, but just look at the men,
slouching toward Florida with crooked teeth!
I have been embarrassed so often by now
I've developed a hump, but
can I look into her eyes and say,
You are average, my dear, only average?
And yet, that's what I love so much,
my heart faints before imperfections,
the sag, wrinkle, distracting blemish:
we are not mannequins, after all.
You have known love and been used hard,
I will say; you were taken to movies
and fuzzy hands groped at your nervous knees.
On public beaches randy twits nuzzled your breasts
while your eyes rolled wildly between ointments.
Maybe this is love, you thought, too generous as usual.
Women have always been generous, even the clothes
you wear a free gift to man
who should kneel down in his baggy pants
and flowered shirt to offer praise. I
will order coffee and sit in supermarkets
all day watching you wheel through
in your shorts and halters, adorable sad faces
twisted in concentration, torn between
canned peaches and pineapple chunks, the store brand
detergent or the trusted Dash. And meat!
How you bend over the counter, hair in your eyes,
puzzling the bloody packages, fatty
content, and artificial coloring.

Oh you should charge a fee for the back of your knees!
I see stories in each line, in each vein
running its startling course. Your son was an angel,
he sells typewriters now, and when you carried
him in your arms his small hands tugged at your
chin and lips, learning the feel of women.
And your daughter, really, looks just like you,
you can see it in the eyes, she tells you
everything when she comes to visit:
men are such children, they are not bad exactly
but sort of warped or frozen like an old movie
at the wrong speed. For my next fifty years
I want to study woman until I open
like a child's hand, like a mother's eye,
like you, love, in your patchwork corner.

About the Author

PETER MEINKE was born in Brooklyn, New York, in 1932. He received his A.B. at Hamilton College, his M.A. at the University of Michigan, and his Ph.D. in Literature at the University of Minnesota. His poems and stories have appeared in *The New Yorker, The Atlantic, The New Republic, Poetry,* and other magazines. His first book of poems, *The Night Train and the Golden Bird,* was published in the Pitt Poetry Series in 1977, and it was followed by *Trying to Surprise God* (1981) and *Night Watch on the Chesapeake* (1987). His first book of stories, *The Piano Tuner,* won the 1986 Flannery O'Connor Award for Short Fiction. A recipient of two Poetry Fellowships from the National Endowment for the Arts, he is Director of the Writing Workshop at Eckard College and lives in St. Petersburg, Florida.

Pitt Poetry Series
Ed Ochester, General Editor

Peter Meinke, *Trying to Surprise God*
Carol Muske, *Applause*
Carol Muske, *Wyndmere*
Leonard Nathan, *Carrying On: New & Selected Poems*
Leonard Nathan, *Holding Patterns*
Sharon Olds, *Satan Says*
Alicia Suskin Ostriker, *Green Age*
Alicia Suskin Ostriker, *The Imaginary Lover*
Greg Pape, *Black Branches*
Kathleen Peirce, *Mercy*
James Reiss, *Express*
David Rivard, *Torque*
William Pitt Root, *Faultdancing*
Liz Rosenberg, *The Fire Music*
Maxine Scates, *Toluca Street*
Richard Shelton, *Selected Poems, 1969–1981*
Peggy Shumaker, *The Circle of Totems*
Arthur Smith, *Elegy on Independence Day*
Gary Soto, *Black Hair*
Gary Soto, *The Elements of San Joaquin*
Gary Soto, *The Tale of Sunlight*
Gary Soto, *Where Sparrows Work Hard*
Tomas Tranströmer, *Windows & Stones: Selected Poems*
Chase Twichell, *Northern Spy*
Chase Twichell, *The Odds*
Leslie Ullman, *Dreams by No One's Daughter*
Constance Urdang, *Alternative Lives*
Constance Urdang, *Only the World*
Ronald Wallace, *The Makings of Happiness*
Ronald Wallace, *People and Dog in the Sun*
Ronald Wallace, *Tunes for Bears to Dance To*
Belle Waring, *Refuge*
Bruce Weigl, *A Romance*
Robley Wilson, *Kingdoms of the Ordinary*
Robley Wilson, *A Pleasure Tree*
David Wojahn, *Glassworks*
David Wojahn, *Mystery Train*
Paul Zimmer, *Family Reunion: Selected and New Poems*